THE RUNYARD FAMILY

Making Up For Lost Time

Published in partnership with Riverside Publishing Solutions.

CONTENTS

FOR BRINGING FAMILIES TOGETHER!

This book is written by the four of us, but we have all written different parts each. We have highlighted these parts throughout, but you will soon learn from the writing styles, who wrote which entry. We will begin with a Prologue by Toby… We hope you enjoy the story. Thanks for reading.

PROLOGUE – *Toby*

You know those fond memories that you have of toddlerhood and pre-school years? Your first birthday parties, those parties that you look back on, that were Toy-Story themed and now just make you cringe? Those memories of your first bike, your first sibling's birth, your first day of school, your first friend (the one you feel you'll be mates with forever, but then you part ways and never, ever see them again). Your first holiday abroad, the flight that you're not sure whether to be afraid of the capsule you're stepping into or to just be amazed at its ability to appear on the land across the seas.

Well, I had all that, as most people do. I had those fond memories. But I didn't have them all with my whole family included. Until 2018, my Dad was a serving member of the Royal Air Force. He wasn't an officer; he was a hard-working (I indeed hope he was!) NCO (non-commissioned officer, a lower ranked service worker), a sergeant to be exact. Being a military worker comes with many positives, such as a good pension, cheaper private school prices for their children, paid travel (although the travel is often to dangerous locations and usually involves working), cheap cooked food in canteens, or in "the mess", and also cheaper housing.

It does, however, come with negatives, which, in my opinion, outweigh the positives. These negatives include having to migrate to different military camps every few years and also having to work abroad.

Having to move home every few years is an action that requires lots of thought from the parents of the family. If a parent is a military worker and is posted to a different camp in the UK, then the family may stay (so the children can stay in their school), although this can clearly separate and break apart the family, or they may move as a whole family and give up most friends and family visits for a while. If the military worker is posted abroad, then the whole family will have to give up everything. In any case, military migration is neither enjoyable nor cheap for any family.

The travelling abroad to work doesn't sound that bad, but when you're the son (or daughter, wife/husband or other friends/family) of someone who has to work abroad for some time, life isn't the same. Now I'm not saying that it's the worst thing that can happen to a family, because some families lose loved ones forever – to whom we owe the greatest sorrows – but being a military family isn't like being a normal family, especially when you're periodically missing a family member.

As children, teenagers and adults, one of the most irritating and upsetting things to have done to you is being given something and then having it immediately snatched away, never to see it again. That's what military life is.

I was born in Oxford, but we moved to Bardney, in Lincolnshire, before I was two. My brother was born in Lincoln and I grew up there until I was seven years old. Then we migrated south to Amesbury, in Wiltshire.

I don't remember Oxford, but I certainly have vivid memories of Lincolnshire. It's a wonderful place, although, admittedly, it is extremely flat (you can see Lincoln Cathedral from miles around because it's on the only hill nearby!). I remember the house being much bigger than our current home (northern houses are cheaper). I can remember my friends and our family friends – there was one family who we were close to called the Kerry's and we've met up with them for small holidays to Wales and the Peak District in recent years. I also remember my school and all the children I knew there. Because of all the things I loved there, which my entire family also loved, the move was pressing and difficult on my family.

However, in Bardney, we were a six-hour drive from my grandparents and extended family, who all resided and still reside in my parents' home county, Somerset. (Somerrrrset, if you want to pronounce it like the locals!) So, moving to Amesbury, where my dad could work at MOD Boscombe Down, meant that our travel journey to grandparents was down to only one hour!

We moved around in Amesbury a lot too! From a military quarter to another and finally into our present home, which doesn't belong to the military. I managed to fit into a new school, but I still missed everything that I used to have. My parents preferred living in Lincolnshire – everything's more spread out, a bit like in America or Australia.

A life lesson I have learnt is "If you don't have the best of everything, make everything you have the best". We did just this and trust me, it worked. My dad continued working in the RAF and my mum continued to work in the NHS as an Orthopaedic Coordinator. My brother and I fitted right into the local Primary School!

Obviously, my life hasn't been anywhere near as upsetting, difficult or as different to 'normal' as many others' lives. Refugees, families of those who are 'lost in battle' and just those who lose a loved one all suffer much more than military families do. However, military families have very different and somewhat more difficult lives than civilian families. Again, this is not entirely true, as some civilian jobs can involve moving around and deployment abroad.

With my dad working abroad on and off for a while though, we had lost a lot of childhood time and experiences with him. The first time he left to work away, I was one year old, so I don't remember that at all. When he went for the second, and final, time, I was five and Adam was two. I remember crossing off every day on a calendar for six months until his return from the Falklands. As only a preschooler, I didn't really know anything about the Falkland Islands. In fact, all I knew was that it wasn't anywhere near where we lived, that it was where Dad was going and had gone, and that it had a lot of penguins. Dad even used to send photos of himself near King Penguins – I was so jealous! He also used to write Blueys (a type of letter that is used as a way of sending letters and messages free to military personnel deployed in certain locations) describing his daily life there, how it was freezing cold and how he missed us. I remember that he used to add a whole line of x's at the end of the letter – that used to make us smile! Sometimes there were enclosed photographs of him at his desk or him working or even of him at the... BAR! (Though we are still not sure to this day if he was *actually* working?) Dad also brought home two King Penguin teddies that Adam and I treasured for many years. All of these different things allowed us to, as far as possible, experience life together: Dad could be 'with' us and we could learn about what he was doing. It was the best we could do to at least pretend to be together.

Before Dad returned, Adam and I had practised making a special cake for him. It came from our favourite show at that time: Big Cook Little Cook. The final cake that we presented to Dad was essentially a chocolate train, consisting of sweets, mini donuts and other additions that made it look a lot more like a train and a lot less like a simple chocolate log, but it had great meaning and was enjoyed greatly by our stomachs.

And yet, there was always something missing between Dad and Adam and I. A missing bond, or a differing humour. Things we didn't know about each other and stories yet to tell. Jokes (the bad ones that dads make) and laughs. Hugs and all good things that make a family – it just wasn't all there.

It was time to make up for this. We decided we'd go on a 'boys only' trip. This book is dedicated to our planning, travelling and experiences on our trip. We hope that other families who lose time with each other because of work, illness or any other reason (whether it be military deployment or civilian) may use this book to encourage them to 'make up lost time'.

AWAY FROM HOME – *Dad*

My first few years as a young adult within the RAF allowed me to travel the world as a technician on the Tristar fleet. I was spoilt early on, by my first posting being with this premier Squadron. Passport, and Samsonite suitcase travelling everywhere – checking in not digging in. Hotels and restaurants, sunbathing, drinking, shopping and nightlife were essentially my career (except when we were travelling). I was certainly fortunate that I hadn't been posted to a helicopter squadron, where they camped in tents, ate rations and got very, very cold at night.

This 'honeymoon period' lasted for some years, enjoying everything the Armed Forces offered, skiing, sports and expeditions. I shared a house (an old quarter no longer fit for family habitat!), life was every young man's dream. Even better, in 2000, the RAF provided us, as a newly married couple, cheap housing, which helped us financially. Sadly, I took Abby away from our home town, but eventually this made us grow stronger together.

It was not until my first detachment to the Falklands (we had our first son, Toby, who was one year old) and another detachment later (we now had our second son, Adam, who was now two years old), that we questioned whether life in the Forces was right for us as a family. It was a time of focus and reflection. Don't get me wrong, I made some good friends whilst I was away and had a good time, but I became concerned that this was time away from my sons that I would never get back.

We decided that a full career would leave us comfortable and able to provide for our young family. However, the cost of all this is moving home a lot and generally being at the call of the RAF. This was a means to an end and we knew we could settle before the boys reached secondary school age and give them a civilian life style from then on.

As a Forces child myself, I am only too aware of the pros and cons of growing up as one: military children tend to make friends more easily and adapt to situations, but having moved around myself this is not the choice we wanted. A quote we learned along the way, "Military children are like flowers; they bloom and grow wherever their roots are put down". The other option for Military children is boarding school, but the funding for this had become harder to acquire.

I don't want to appear ungrateful: I signed on the dotted line and I have had a good time and been afforded many opportunities. It has provided for my family, but the Forces have changed and a lot has changed in me, from that teenager walking into the Careers Office (Recruiting Centre).

THE IDEA - *Dad*

The 'Boys trip' had been a seed in my head for a few years. It was going to be my time with just the children, making up for all the precious 'first moments' I'd missed out on. I'd spent so much time away from home on detachment or away on courses during my twenty-two years RAF service, that the thought of touring the UK with my two young boys had kept me going. All the nights and weekends I'd spent alone in one-man room accommodation or in secluded, bleak accommodation in the Falkland Islands would all disappear once I hit the road with Toby and Adam.

My original thoughts were that we'd purchase three open train tickets – so we could jump on and off train stations all over the UK – stopping and camping wherever we ended up and cooking on a campfire. This would incorporate copious amounts of walking whilst carrying all our kit. My experience as an Assistant Cub Leader, left me undeterred – I had gone on many camping trips, most without any drama, although there was one camp that was held on a very wet, rainy weekend in November. So wet, that one of our Cubs slipped and fell in the mud, hitting his head, resulting in a trip to A&E and early collection by his parents. Not so successful. But I had been camping and walking with my little family, so why wouldn't this work?

Whilst I thought this was going to be the best trip since Christopher Columbus discovered America, my wife had serious doubts about my capabilities of coping with two young children, three sets of kit plus a tent and three sleeping bags, whilst getting on and off trains, walking along roads to the nearest campsite, pitching up and then cooking enough food (my cooking skills are very limited even in the home) to feed three potentially ravenous and exhausted humans. My wife pointed out the predictability of the English summer weather and how we'd probably be traipsing around the countryside in torrential rain, that we'd all come down with colds, the tent would probably leak, clothes wouldn't dry out, blisters… her list of 'what ifs' were endless. But I had to admit, my wife had a point. And of course, having single-parented our children whilst I was away all that time, had left her far more qualified as a parent than me. During both of my tours of the Falklands, she had cared for the children on her own, with short breaks to and from her parents', whilst holding down a part-time job in the NHS. And gradually reality struck. I knew only too little of the issues that could arise: homesickness, tiredness, 'I don't want to walk anymore!' It would only take a small issue such as these to bring the whole trip to an abrupt halt. And could we really carry all the food, or in reality – could I really carry all their food along with everything else, once they'd had enough of 'look at how much I can carry compared to him'? Every moment I had some spare time, I would look into other possibilities of how this could work. Ideas including taking RAF ten-man ration packs – the boys would have them – they contained YORKIES ('not for girls') and 'brown biscuits to bung you up'! (Only those in the know, know what these are).

Originally, the aim was to get to the end of my career then head off travelling with the boys. But as I entered my last two years, the consideration that perhaps my priority at the end of my military career should probably be focusing on pursuing another career started to take place. I might actually be having job interviews or undertaking work experience, might even still be panicking about not having a job. This worry might ruin the UK trip. It therefore became apparent that I should bring the trip forward and go the year before I left whilst I was still getting paid. Doing it at this time also fitted in with 11+ preparation for my oldest son.

After many long family discussions and research, we decided that our mode of transport should be the iconic VW Campervan, mainly down to its ease of use, space, dryness, and mattresses (compared to camping roll mats and tents).

MILITARY PLANNING – *Dad*

Having decided we were going by campervan we had great difficulty deciding which model to go for... old and classic versus modern and spacious? Many a website was visited, trying to pick a local company for our transport. One son wanted to travel classic, the other wanted to go fast and furious. The need for reliability took priority so we chose modern, fast and furious. With the theme of fast and furious in our heads, we found a company that hired modern campervans (but also Lambos, Mustangs, DB9S and Ferraris – we are Top Gear followers). So, drawn into the Lambos' and DB9s that this company hired, we went to specify the details and check out the vehicle that would become our home for three weeks. After *more* discussing with the Company Director, this became our choice and a deposit was put down. Knowing we now had our transport sorted we began to lay down the **blueprints**...

Where did we want to go to? Which route would we take? How far would we travel each day? There were so many

Campervan vs Mustang?

decisions to make and we all had different opinions on it all. We had to focus on what we were looking at gaining from the trip and that was quality time together, doing 'boy things' and getting an education along the way. We'd previously been to Land's End, so travelling that far south wasn't required. We were heading… North. Our aim… to reach the furthest point in mainland Scotland – Dunnet Head (not John O'Groats as is commonly thought). Now, which route would we take? Surrounding our UK map laid out on the floor, the three of us pinpointed areas that would be our points of interest, again, we all had different favourites… old and classic son wanted to visit churches and cathedrals, fast and furious son wanted football and rugby stadiums. I wanted peaceful and scenic settings. More compromising was required. On reflection, this part of the process was probably the hardest and most problematic part. With such a huge area of options and a variety of individual interests, a lot of time was spent deciding on one place then undeciding ten minutes later. We also had to factor in journey times. As I was going to be the sole *driver*, I didn't particularly want to be driving for longer than 4 hours a day especially as I would be the sole *parent* along the way too. We all know how testing some journeys can be with young children. Not all our holidays in the past had had successful and joy-filled journeys, and my wife had been on all these trips so we'd shared the load! Or rather, I'd taken the driver's seat while my wife had entertained the kids and kept them fed and watered from beginning to end. So, knowing that I was to be the driver, entertainer **and parent**, I had to bear in mind the energy this would zap from me. I didn't want to be 'grumpy Dad' while on this once-in-a-lifetime trip.

It probably took a month of planning before we came up with a final route; evenings after school and work were spent sitting on the floor next to the opened-up map so we could all see. We bought dot stickers and highlighters to mark our way around the UK, peeling them off and replacing them if we changed the route. Our next task was to choose and book the campsites. Having had a caravan in the past, I knew I wanted at least the standard of Caravan Club sites: I had to be guaranteed a decent shower and toilet if we were travelling for three weeks. No way was I wanting to slum it... until my 'fast and furious' son spotted a wild camping site – advertised as a 'shovel given on arrival' campsite – my young son was won over and had his toilet roll ready to pack. My 'old and classic' son was frantically and nervously planning how he would arrange his wild, outdoor bathroom facilities for maximum comfort. I, however, was just not thinking about it. Knowing now we had a rough and ready campsite, we needed to book a 5*, luxurious, comfortable top-end campsite. We found the perfect spot for this at Edinburgh. This planning continued until our final campsite was chosen and booked at our final destination, in sunny Devon, next to the glorious sea. This would be where we would stay for a week and be joined by my wife, Abby. Images of being relieved from my parental duties as soon as Abby arrived were foremost at this point!

THE FINAL PLAN

TRIP AROUND THE UK

<table>
<tr><td>Monday 24</td><td>PEAK DISTRICT
Sheffield Poolsbrook Country Park Caravan Club Site S43 3WL No fires.</td></tr>
<tr><td>Tuesday 25</td><td>ANGEL OF NORTH (NE9 7TY)
Brockwell wood NE21 6JR. Fires allowed. Logs, kindling and three burgers requested. 1500 arrival.</td></tr>
<tr><td>Wednesday 26</td><td>EDINBURGH
Drummohr Holiday Park EH21 8JS 27. No fires.</td></tr>
<tr><td>Thursday 27</td><td rowspan="2">AVIEMORE
Glenmore Camping, PH22 1QU. No fires.</td></tr>
<tr><td>Friday 28</td></tr>
</table>

Saturday 29	**JOHN O GROATS** KW1 4YR 01955 611329.
Sunday 30	**BEN NEVIS**
Monday 31	PH33 6SX.
Tuesday 1 Aug	**GLASGOW** Galloway forest park, Mount View Caravan Park, Abington, South Lanarkshire, Scotland, **ML12 6RW**
Wednesday 2	Windermere Stop at Hadrian's Wall (**CA8 7DD**) **LA22 0HY**
Thursday 3	**WINDERMERE GRIZDALE** Grizedale forest **LA22 0QJ**
Friday 4	**LIVERPOOL** Chester Fairoaks Caravan Club Site, Rake Lane, Little Stanney, Chester, Cheshire, **CH2 4HS**
Saturday 5	**BRECONS** Aberbran Fawr Farm **LD3 9NG**
Sunday 6	**BRECONS** Fires allowed.
Monday 7	**CROYDE** **EX3 31NY**

Route planned, campervan booked, campsites booked – what did we need to plan next? Of course, the most important necessity – food – needed for our well-being throughout. This had to be healthy but with some tasty snacks to keep us going. Quick and convenient was also required. So, the following list was drawn up:

Boys' Choice	**Mum's Choice**
• Coco pops • Crisps • Chocolate • Chips • Fish fingers • Pot noodles • Super noodles • Burgers • Tinned All day breakfast • Cafes • Hot chocolate • Sweets • Coke	• Bran flakes • Fruit • Vegetables • Carrot sticks • Cucumber sticks • Cheese • Tuna (not for me: I don't like fish!) • Bottled water • Milk • Pasta • John o' Groats – celebratory fish and chips

So, after loads of discussion about healthy eating versus convenience, we came up with a combined list of the two choices, heavily weighted by Mums' choice. Abby wouldn't sleep knowing I was feeding rubbish to the boys, and I didn't want any digestive problems. I thought we'd take a contingency cash flow for emergency refreshment breaks and for the occasions where we saw a nice coffee shop or fast-food restaurant (this was the boys' secret from Mum).

Next, what clothing did we need to take? Light, comfy and easy to wash in campsite laundrettes. Not smart nor expensive or requires ironing. That was easy planning.

Then, what games/activities would we take? As we all know, children these days only look out of the car window for a limited time, preferring to absorb themselves in electronics or big headphones and music, watching YouTube and various other trash on the internet. But of course, this wasn't what I wanted from this trip and didn't think the boys would gain anything from doing that all the way, so I decided that electronics would be very limited in use*, and I would opt for the 'look at the view' kind of entertainment but also suggested card games. Toby and Adam chose some varying Top Trumps and card games. Abby suggested back to basic colouring and drawing, but that didn't appeal to any of us – neither boys are particularly keen and I didn't have faith that the colours would avoid the van's upholstery and then I'd be left with having to scrub the upholstery, probably unsuccessfully, leaving me minus the deposit paid for the van. We planned to get books from the library, a journal for daily record keeping and maybe an audio book or two. A rugby ball was top of the list and a cricket set was going in too plus the latest fad – Kendama. We looked forward to spending time outside together, making friends with other families and enjoying the fresh air and views.

**I would reserve electronic time for the moments of driving where it was either chaotic with traffic jams or if I was lost and needed to concentrate. With my navigation and map reading skills, I was confident this would not happen too often. But also reserved for those times, when they would be too tired to be civil to each other and separation was necessary for our sanity.*

By now, the trip was looking very real. Our plans were made. We were now waiting patiently for the time to arrive when we collected the van, packed it up and headed off into the sunset – well, our plan was to set off at sunrise, but that doesn't sound as magical.

DAY 0: PREPARATION – *Dad*

Finally, the day to collect the campervan arrived. To say we were excited was an understatement: the boys were hyper, even the sensible one. I hadn't slept all night, constantly thinking our plan over and over. We jumped into our car as early as we could and headed off to 'Drive South West'. This company was run by an enthusiastic group of guys, who clearly had a love of all road-able vehicles. They worked from a not so glamorous trading estate but once you'd seen the cars they were letting out; the location was irrelevant. The campervan was outside their lock-up when we got there. It was gleaming in the sun. They'd obviously spent some time preparing it and it looked A-mazing, especially with the also gleaming Ferrari parked behind it. So, Derek – one of the company partners- gave us a familiarisation session. I listened carefully, while my wife was pretending to be interested – she has never been into vehicles or packing, so listening to someone telling us about every last bit of storage in the campervan was not enjoyable for her! The boys were listening to the bits that interested them – mainly the practical side of things – how the roof expanded, how the roof bed was erected and so on. We all listened carefully to the breakdown procedure (one of my fears of the trip) and attention was paid to the Ad-Blue and diesel tank. Thankfully, the boys were not trampling all over the seats, although I did catch them sitting on the front passenger seat and swivelling it around like a waltzer at a fair. My wife was busy securing Adam's child car seat to the rear seat, safety first, and I was working out the sat nav. The handover was completed and we were handed the keys. Time to jump in and begin the fun. Obviously, the boys wanted to come with me in the van, while my wife drove home alone... We still weren't quite there yet though, we had to get home to pack the van up and wait for departure day, the next morning.

The journey home was fun, we all began to become acquainted with our 'home' for the next few weeks. The van drove well and I adapted to it without problems. The boys talked excitedly about it and were fiddling cautiously with bits and pieces.

CAMPERVAN SPEC – *Adam*

Now, for the beauty of the campervan: a T6 VW Transporter to be exact. With a sporty trim and dark interior, it is sleek; it's full of cool tech such as a swivelling passenger chair, a satnav and a kitchenette with everything you need! It has enough room to sleep four people. But the most impressive bit – the pop-up roof converting into a comfortable double bed with a window to look out of whilst you drift off to sleep, to see the stunning views.

But... it doesn't stop there. It has a 2L engine capable of creating a wonderful 145 horsepower. It has four quick working cylinders and can do an impressive 39mpg and finally the top speed is 126mph. It is one of the best and most comfortable and compact campervans today.

Dad

As soon as we got home, we wanted to crack on with packing – my wife was equally happy with this, as our narrow hallway had increasingly become our trip's storage area! Getting in and out of the front door had become a bit of an obstacle course. I thought my wife may have been a bit apprehensive and about us leaving and therefore happy to have our clutter in her way, but on reflection, I think she may have been looking forward to the squash and squeeze effect (if you've ever read the Julia Donaldson children's book, you know what I mean). So, adhering to our storage plan, bit by bit, the van was loaded. We all had our own plastic stackable Ikea box for clothes which tucked into the boot nicely. The food went in the cupboards and fridge. The bedding went up onto the bunk, and yes, the boys practiced preparing the push-up roof and getting their bed ready. They sorted out where the activities were going. I programmed some favourite radio channels in and got my head around the sat nav. My wife checked the fruit and veg had gone in, plus the toiletries and first aid kit. My wife had also printed and A4 poly-pocketed our journey plan, campsite booking confirmations/receipts and emergency telephone numbers. This all went into the glove compartment for safe keeping. Abby went inside the house to vacuum the cleared hallway.

Bedtime then fast approached. We each had a bubbly, hot bath – our last proper wash, no doubt, for a while. We had a fulfilling home cooked meal, no doubt our last for a while. And before we went to bed, we had a massive family hug, again, our last for a while. We were then all ready for the big adventure ahead.

DAY 1

05.30 – alarm clock buzzing. The boy's trip around the UK was about to begin. I'd set the alarm but to be honest, I'd been awake for a while, eager to get up and get on the road. I'd been planning this for so long now, this was the moment to make up for lost time while I'd been working away from home, missing out on father/son moments. This was where I'd really get to know them again, as individuals and as sons. We were going to share some special times together to create memories we could hold on to for years to come.

Once up and dressed, my wife and I woke up the boys. They both simultaneously jumped out of bed and got dressed, each as excited as a dog being shown its lead. Or was it that whoever got out to the van first, got to travel up front with me? Quick goodbyes to Mum (proper goodbyes had been said the night before), she handed me an envelope and asked one of the boys to open it and read it an hour into the journey. Toby tucked it into the side pocket, I imagined a long letter explaining what we should and shouldn't be doing, things to remember to do, safety advice etc. To our surprise when Toby opened it, he revealed a simple note 'treat yourselves to your first and last fast-food breakfast', also enclosed was a £10 note. Winner! McDonalds here we come! Thank you very much Mum!

We made it to the first campsite in record time – thanks to the early start! This first night would set the precedence of the rest of our trip together. Now was the time to set camp duties and boundaries so we all knew what was expected.

To keep things simple, this first stop was a motorhome and caravan club, called Poolsbrook Country Park Caravan Club Site. With Caravan Club sites you get a set standard of facilities. They tend to be the same high standard, the Premier Inn equivalent I guess, without the guaranteed mattress. As such, the pitch was large and level, we had washing up facilities, a sports field, shower facilities, an adventure playground and at this campsite we even had an enormous lake to walk around!

When we arrived, little had to be said, the boys jumped out of the van, watched me reverse, and before I had the handbrake on, they were putting the roof up and making their room for the night. This was not one of those holidays where you set up, put the awning up and get everything out. We deliberately kept it simple, so we could enjoy the time together.

So off we went for a walk to explore and relieve some energy and excitement.

It wasn't long, before Toby had reported back that the facilities were ok; this became his very important job at every campsite. (Thankfully, to mine and Adams relief, he only once reported them being dirty, this was in Scotland. On venturing to the shower later to investigate his claims, we discovered his allegation was false and was merely caused by the eerie presence of some crane flies which had taken over the ceiling!)

Hungry, I returned to the van, to put dinner on. We had filled the campervan with food prior to leaving and had planned meals. Simple meals to be cooked on a single hob and/or grill were planned with the boys so they could have ownership. I cooked for tonight whilst they explored and played football with other children.

Whilst the boys went to wash up in the campsite facilities (as the sink in the van was only suitable for breakfast plates and cups), I cleared up, put the table away and prepared for some indoor/outdoor games. This included throwing the rugby ball around and also a game of cards which became the decider for who would butter the bread each day to have with dinner – lots of fresh air and exercise results in very hungry boys!

Now our routine was set: shower, teeth and bed at around 2100. This gave me an inverse lie in, and meant we could all be freshly awake and ready for the next day's adventures!

■ Our first and most favourite photo of the trip

7 WVV

DAY 2

As the boys packed up the following morning and put the roof down on what was their bedroom, a little technique was needed (and muscle), to pull the roof down but also not to catch the canvas. This was soon mastered and another job that I was no longer needed for.

Toby and Adam were far more capable than I had imagined; they were like young adults. It felt like they had gone from the early days of needing to be fed and changed; to being fed again, through to toilet training, more feeding then to being carried; learning to walk all the way to where they are now: the 'we don't need you' attitude! This reminds me of a book given to me by one of our neighbours, she was a midwife (not our midwife) and she lent me a book called '60 min father'. The book sets goals to help every father ensure that he doesn't miss out on the greatest opportunity of his life – advice includes such things as writing letters when you're away from the family home. Also, that you generally only have the time from your child's birth to when they become teenagers to bond with your children. For the parent that must work away during the week, it gives some ideas to enhance their parent bond. For some military families this fits, i.e. those that work away for extended periods or those on shift work. Some military families decide that living near their extended family – rather than near the base is more beneficial – this is definitely a plus side when children come along, as you have support close by for childcare! Either way, time away from home is time lost bonding. Some other suggestions in the book can be adapted for longer time away, on detachment. But most of all, the book explained in detail that those who show love, care and interest in their children tend to have the feelings reciprocated later on in life!

Back to the trip: the first morning – breakfast, roof down, chocks away, pull up to the water filling station on the way out where boys filled our water tank . . . and off we go – a smooth military operation . . . this was how our mornings rocked.

Every trip needs a song and ours turned out to be Despacito by Luis Fonsi. This tune was being played on most local radio stations as we toured. Had it been sung in English I don't think Abby would have been too impressed with our nine and twelve-year old learning the lyrics. Luckily the boys didn't understand the Spanish language at the time! So, every time we heard the tune, the sunglasses went on, windows went down and we belted it out. What is it about a good sing along in the car – it always guarantees a good time feeling?

Now, whilst the idea was to just have time together, one also likes to educate one's children along life's path.

And after a couple of hours drive, it was time to stop for lesson No.1 – Angel of the North – object of lesson: to find out what it was, why it was there and how long had it been there for? We also needed lunch, and a bit of fresh air.

Angel of the North

With a wingspan of over 50 metres, the whole Angel weighs over 200 tonnes (108 for the body and 50 for each wing). The reason it was there: because nobody has ever seen one so "we need to keep believing"!

The Angel of the North

Sadly, we can't recommend this café as Dad said he hadn't budgeted to stop at every café along the way – not even the last one in England.

Successful lesson completed and with a snack of carrots in hand, we started up again on the A1.

Crossing the Scottish border was a milestone! We made a quick stop for the photo opportunity. The boys then carried on playing a couple of card games, reading their books and talking (I think it was about farming – or at least that's what I picked up – and it involved all the misinformation that children pick up here and there). Soon enough we reached the next campsite. This campsite was within an immense site full of woods and fields and more woods. It was huge! Excitedly, the boys ran off and got lost in the acres of land, finding rope swings on the way. This campsite, however, was slightly, if not very, bizarre. This was one of Scotland's infamous wild camping sites – one that Adam had chosen when planning. We had booked it for a bit of fun for the sole reason that no toilets were provided! It would have been alright for the campervans or caravans that have toilets within them (but these tend to be longer, therefore manouvering them around this site would most likely be impossible due to the tight bends), but this campsite was designed for tents and small campervans without toilets, like the one that we were in. The campsite, instead of providing facilities, provided shovels, which were to be used to dig holes for, yes, you know what! My young and messy son couldn't be bothered to dig a hole in advance, he thought he would simply dig it when the time for needing it arrived and it was this that he later came to regret when he ran out of time to dig a hole, as I had tried to warn him! My elder son, however, prepared as

Wild camping (only in Scotland)

soon as we arrived, so he was ready in case he needed one, which he ironically didn't in the end!

The boys carried on playing, one came back for a bit, blaming the other for getting them hurt, but then he ran off to play again, so he can't really have been hurt can he... They played in a cornfield as well, so they both came back with scratches on their legs, but they didn't mind. As the sun began to set, we ate fresh beef burgers, which I'd like to mention, came fresh from the onsite farm – another point that drew us in to picking this site as one of our stays. These were, honestly, some of the best burgers that I have ever purchased: they were meaty, juicy and full of flavour, not that I'm a critic or anything! We buried potatoes deep inside our fire, wrapped in tin foil, so they weren't crispy on the outside. For a delicious pudding we melted some giant marshmallows on our flaming fire! After this sumptuous, locally sourced meal, we felt stuffed, so it wasn't long before we all wanted to get to bed. Pitched deep within the forest, we lay in our sleeping bags and listened out to the night time sounds unfamiliar to us – trees rustling, wolves howling, deer prancing, bears stomping, – amazing what you can lead the children to believe they can hear!

DAY 3 – *Toby*

Day 3 was, again, another day being woken up by the freezing cold, but because we had woken up just a bit earlier than necessary, we all sat in bed and read together. After only a minute or two, we had breakfast: a bowl of the same cereal (we were already bored of the same cereal, so there's nothing exciting to say about this!). Off we set on Day 3 of our journey! After many a stop for toilet breaks and more carrot snacking, we reached Edinburgh – a place of castles and cold temperatures. Our predetermined route took us straight past Edinburgh Castle, but consequentially, this route led us to city traffic and we were stuck in it for a long time – a very long time indeed! For me and Adam, this meant more card games (which for some reason we never got bored of, probably because we were being very competitive) and for Dad it meant sitting and waiting, more sitting and waiting, until we eventually escaped and managed to weave around the outskirts of the city to reach Drummohr Holiday Park, our destination for the night.

Leaderfoot Viaduct

Dad needed to stretch his legs, so after pitching up, we left immediately to go on a semi-walk, semi-run tour of the area (we were almost too tired, but not quite too tired to run). There was an extremely windy beach not far from the campsite, so we ran along the coastal path, stopping to read the information signs and hence learning that we were actually staying in an area of Edinburgh called Musselburgh, which was once covered in mines, hence some towers and the odd quarry that we spotted along the way. On our way back, we managed to get lost, 1 km extra added to our run to be exact; I blame the map reader, which thankfully wasn't me!

When we finally got back to the van, I offered to cook dinner, because, after all, like most dads, my dad is pretty

■ A remote snack break

terrible in the kitchen and even worse when you only have one hob and one mini oven to use. I prepared a delicious spag bol, but just as I finished, we ran out of gas, so Dad and Adam ran off to the campsite's shop hoping and praying that it was still open, as it was rather late. A good chef should properly taste his food – to ensure it tastes phenomenal – so I also made sure that I did this, but seeing as Dad and Adam were gone, I had just a little bit more than necessary... Then I heard something driving around outside and looked up only to see Adam and Dad having fun on the back of a golf buggy! Oh, how I wish that I'd gone with them! They explained, whilst connecting up the new gas canisters, that the shop had just been closing as they arrived, but that the kind manager let them in and he even gave them a ride back in his buggy!

Before nightfall, we all used the site's showers, but as every person who has used any campsite's showers ever will know, they are always either too hot or too cold, there's never a "Goldilocks' temperature". But we used them and were at least clean for another day...

DAYS 4 AND 5

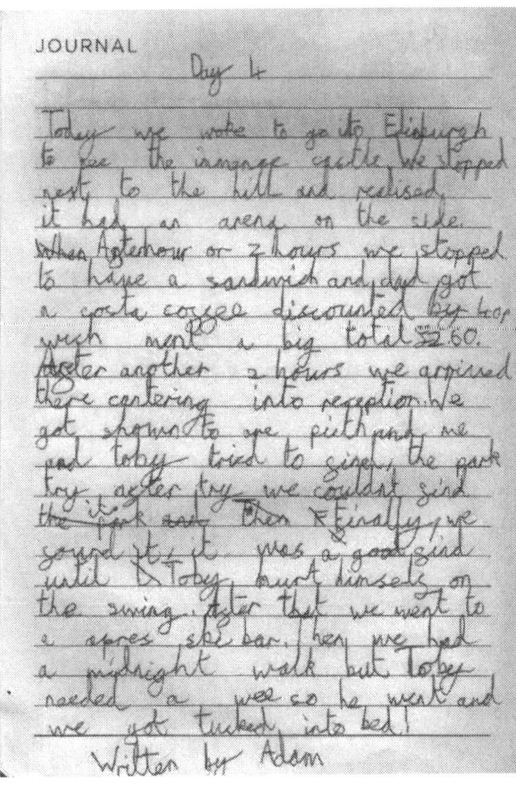

JOURNAL

Day 4

Today we woke to go ito Edinburgh
to see the immense castle. We stopped
next to the hill and realised
it had an arena on the side.
~~When~~ After an hour or 2 hours we stopped
to have a sandwich and dad got
a costa coffee discounted by 40p
wich meant a big total £2.60.
After another 2 hours we arrived
there entering into reception. We
got shown to our pitch and we
and Toby tried to find the park
try after try we couldn't find
~~the park and~~ it Then Finally, we
found it, it was a good find
until Toby hurt himself on
the swing. After that we went to
a apres ski bar. Then we had
a midnight walk but Toby
needed a wee so he went and
we got tucked into bed!

Written by Adam

The next two days were great fun. We drove straight to Aviemore, a town nestled in the Cairngorms, a beautiful mountainous area in Scotland where we sometimes go skiing, but as it was the summer, we obviously couldn't. I've been going to this amazingly beautiful location since I was very young and because I've only been there in the winter, I only ever remember it as a snowy, windy place, so I was pleasantly surprised to find it warm and sunny (of course, I wasn't expecting snow, but it was actually very, very warm for a Scottish town set in the mountains), so its lucky that during planning, we decided to book two nights at the campsite here! The campsite was set on the shore of the small Loch Morlich and all I can say is that I love Aviemore more than ever for what I saw here: the loch, which can freeze and ice over in parts some winters, was covered in sailboats, engine boats, wakeboarders, paddle boarders, kayakers and even windsurfers – it was alive! Now, you might expect this of a lake in summer, but what made me smile was the fact that Aviemore was so adaptable and could, each year, turn from a skiing town, with invitingly warm and cosy cafes, ski slopes and slopes perfect for sledging, to a summer paradise, with mountain climbing, water sports, beach-side sunbathing and even a forest, ideally suited for mountain biking.

I couldn't wait to spend time here. So as soon as we arrived, we set up the campervan and then Adam and I ditched Dad and ran off to the park for a bit (with a walkie-talkie in case we had to contact Dad – they're far more fun than a mobile phone!) The park, however, was very difficult to find, and after trying and trying we just could not find it. Then we realised that we needed to go **through** the campsite's immense forest and not around it. The park in question was like one of those mini-adventure obstacle courses, except that at the end, there was one of those swings that looks like a large net. Soon enough, however, to Dad's expectance, we ended up running back when one of us managed to get hurt. For once though, we didn't start blaming each other. I had been hit by the swing and I admitted to falling below it as Adam swung above me. I had lifted up my head only for the swing to knock me straight back down, so in this case it was me being somewhat stupid. Oh boys, what are we like!?...

The first time we've visited Aviemore outside of the skiing season. What a contrast the summer landscape was!

As our location was a special place for us, we decided we should, after having an enjoyable dinner at a nearby après-ski bar, go on a midnight walk. The lake, which lay next to the campsite, reflected the nearby mountains and the moon too, so the walk seemed very powerful. I seem to remember that it featured in my dreams that night, but dreams are very hard to remember after all.

We knew, as soon as we woke up purposefully early the next day, that it was to be an exciting one, as we had one whole day in Aviemore and we had a lot to do. First, we had a chore to complete: we each carried some of our dirty clothes across to the campsite's laundry room. It doesn't sound like a lot of effort and you're right it really wasn't, but it was still a necessary chore. We read for half an hour when we got back to the van and then returned to the laundry room, where we were lucky to find that another camper had bought too much time on a tumble drier, so she let us use the remainder of her time for our wet washing. Whilst we waited for this time to finish, we went to rent out some mountain bikes – we were again very lucky as the shop keeper said he would let us have them till the next morning but we only paid for the one day. To further my thoughts about Aviemore managing to thrive biannually, we found out that the shopkeeper was, in winter, a ski instructor on the mountain, so we listened to him talk about this for a while and told him about our winter experiences here too. What an incredible guy he was!

We collected our clothes and hung them out, as they weren't quite dry yet and then we began our bike ride...

After five miles of rocky terrain and flat out cycling up steep roads, we made it to our first destination – the ski slope. This was a truly sad sight for us, as it was totally empty of people (we could, for some reason, walk into the fitting room for skis which is usually full to the brim of patient yet eager skiers waiting to be fitted for skis and ski boots) and what was usually covered in a blanket of snow was just a plain, grey, rocky surface. The ski lifts hung, swinging in the wind, in a strangely ghostly fashion. It was as if someone had "sucked the spirit out of the Cairngorms". One plus side of being up here, though, was the view – it was breath-taking. We could, quite literally, see for miles and miles and miles. We could see the other mountains nearby, more Lochs in the distance and we could make out just about how far the pine forests went.

We took a couple of photos of the view, plus a selfie for Mum, before we turned back and began a speedy descent back down the mountain. We whizzed back down the roads and as we passed our campsite, we slowed and came off the road and onto the official mountain biking path that would take us straight back into town. It was bumpy and gravelly (so perfect for some skidding practice). There were even a few proper jumps for us to have a go at, which we did and enjoyed greatly. Adam and I are very competent cyclists, but this was our first time doing actual mountain biking, so we followed Dad around some cool tracks and tried not to get too cocky. We eventually arrived, exhausted, on the outskirts of Aviemore and we had to race through the town because it began to pour with rain as we headed to our favourite café, the Mountain View Café. We always go here whenever we visit Aviemore, as the staff and café itself are very welcoming, but mainly because the food is absolutely delicious and the coffees and teas are perfect for Mum and Dad too. I managed to bag the last Blueberry and White Chocolate Scone, which made Dad very envious as it looked and smelled flavoursome, but he found some other inviting cakes, so I didn't feel *too* bad.

Whilst letting our food go down and waiting for the rain to pass, we walked under the cover of shops down the high street towards the chemist's. Although not previously mentioned, I had, for the last day or two, had a sore spot under my right eye and it had grown, become much itchier and turned bright red, so I asked in the chemist what to do about it. It turns out that it was a type of lump called a *stye*, which is *"a bacterial infection of an oil gland in the eyelid. This results in a red tender bump at the edge of the eyelid."* (That is the online definition, but it's exactly as the chemist described it). The chemist then said that each morning and evening I should (and this is what I did for the next week) soak a flannel in warm water and hold it on my eye for 5 minutes. This would draw out the oiliness of the spot and would therefore deflate it. Thankfully this turned out to work and I haven't had anything similar since and I continue to wash my face every day in the hope that I don't get it in the future.

Stunning area for cycling

Once the rain had stopped, we cycled back to Loch Morlich and spent the afternoon cycling around the forest that surrounded it. This was great fun, as there were smaller trails that we followed that lead off from the main one. There was one incident where Dad came down a steep slope, but Adam and I were in the way, so he had to stop suddenly and he genuinely skidded over a banana skin, which was coincidently and inconveniently for him, placed right in his track. We were annoyed that someone had actually left it there, but at least it wasn't damaging litter, which we actually saw none of on our ride.

We finished the day by searching for a fish and chip shop – we needed a reward for cycling around for an entire day. We ended up heading to a nearby youth hostel and enjoyed some of their fish and chips on the edge of the loch, before we headed back to our camper for a good night's sleep.

A SCOTTISH TOWN – *Dad*

As a keen skier myself, fortunately skiing from school age and then in later years able to ski with the RAF, I wanted my family to experience the freedom of the slopes. Abby had already endured this escapade, however, now in the later years of our twenty-year marriage, she has informed me that skiing and the cold is not really her thing. I would like to take this moment to say thank you to her, for at least pretending that our honeymoon to Banff in Canada was fun!

Aviemore holds a particular special place in our hearts. When the boys were of really young age, and I had just returned from a detachment in the Falkland Islands, we took them to a 'chalet' in Aviemore. The small town resembles a quiet ski resort with all its enticing outdoor shops, its lovely coffee shops and a number of après-ski bars. However, to a four-year-old, the real excitement is the noise and thrill of the funicular railway, which ends with spectacular views at the peak of the Cairngorm Mountains.

Now, the Cairngorms are not renowned for **excellent** ski slopes, in fact the snow is more of an ice rink! Not to mention the chill factor with the ever-strong wind. However, at the stage of the boys' skiing they knew no better. It was also affordable and offered a great opportunity for me to teach them the basics. And if you can ski in the conditions that Scotland throws at you, then you can ski anywhere – right?!

DAY 6 – THE MOST NORTHERLY POINT – *Adam*

'We have this envelope for you and we have been waiting a few days to find out what it is?', the lady behind the counter at the campsite reception handed over the letter to us, with a very inquisitive look. (Dad will explain more about this in a bit).

Our drive into John o'Groats was very strange because about an hour from the town, the roads became very quiet. There were barns and buildings that were derelict, and cars that had fallen apart too, but everything was so far apart as well, as if this place was abandoned, like a warzone. Then, as we got to about ten minutes away, everything suddenly brightened up again. As roads from across Scotland seemed to join together, we saw people walking with back-packs, cyclists with panniers and hundreds of campervans on the roads. Many of these people were completing the Land's End to John o'Groats journey. *Others had taken the famous Scottish equivalent of USA's Route 66 – a 516-mile route around the North Coast of Scotland beginning and ending at*

Inverness Castle. It was officially named as NC500 (North Coast 500) in 2015 and soon described by many as "one of the most beautiful coastal touring routes in the world". We even saw an amazingly inspiring, very elderly man walking alone, who we overtook in the van on the way, only to be passed by him when we stopped for lunch. His t-shirt claimed he was walking from Lands End and Toby and I couldn't believe it, we thought that he must have been crazy!

We were now at our most northerly campsite in John o'Groats, the most northerly town in mainland Britain, not to be confused with Dunnet Head the most northerly point, which we visited later.

Another 'first' for us, was the sight of a ginormous sleeper-bus, which had driven over from France and was so large, it must have had a hundred people on board! It had an entire trailer the size of another bus for luggage, food and cooking!

***

Dad

As we settled in to this small, but adequate, campsite looking out to the Orkney Islands, one wonders what more one could want in life. The campsite had an air of excitement where the children felt free. We were invited for drinks with the foreign neighbours, where we shared anecdotes of travels.

'You've made it!' – stated the 'Congratulations' card from Abby, the envelope the campsite receptionist had been so interested in. It included money for an ice cream too! Abby had posted the note a few days earlier. We all had a little moment, thinking of Abby/Mum and missing her an incy bit! But we had to move on… since we'd already treated ourselves to chips that night, the boys put Abby's money towards trying a portion of haggis. As expected, Adam, my youngest didn't like it at all and made that exaggerating face of disgust that most children do when they think they've been poisoned by food presented by their parents, whilst my eldest said 'it's alright, a bit weird, but alright'. In addition to the haggis, Adam was overly impressed by the chippy's square burgers, which was something he'd never seen!

Dunnet Head is the most Northerly Point of mainland UK and is also one of the most beautiful places, in my opinion, in the UK as well. From here you can see the Duncan by Stacks to the East, Cape Wrath to the West and North to Orkney. In fact, just 6.75 miles from Dunnet Head is the nearest point in the Orkney Islands, so, when we drove here after dinner, we could see them clearly amongst the vast horizon above the Atlantic Ocean / North Sea. The lighthouse is 20m high placed on an 85m high cliff making it 105m above sea level, so it stands overly tall and is therefore extremely useful for ships returning at night or in storms even to this day.

Upon returning to the campsite, I asked Toby to check the showers and utilities to see if they were clean, as we had already encountered some disgustingly dirty bathrooms on our trip. He came back and said that it was covered in insects and didn't look nice at all, so we gave showers a miss that evening, only to find out soon after (and too late to have showers) that just one or two moths and Daddy Longlegs spiders (actually named Cellar Spiders) were what had put him off. The showers were, ironically, apart from the odd insect, the nicest I had seen in a while, as they were in their own individual cubicles and not just separated by thin high-pressure laminate sheets, as in plenty of public toilets and campsite shower rooms.

And as I sat back and watched the sun go down (which was really late at this northern point) all was well with the world! Birds flew, dipping and diving, over the sea, the waves were crashing sleepily and the clouds hung still. I felt as though I was in the perfect setting for a book about the coast. Everything was still and everything was quiet, well, that wasn't true, because Adam and Toby had decided to go and hang out with our previously mentioned Polish neighbours. So, instead of watching this perfect scene across the sea, I felt obliged to talk more with the Dutch adults, whilst the boys took part in sword fights and played tag with two of the Polish boys – Olaf and Isaac were their names, I believe. After what must have been almost two hours (I hadn't wanted to call the boys in due to the amount of fun they had seemed to be having) they returned to the van tired and mucky from whatever fighting game they had been playing. They waved goodbye to the neighbouring

Dunnet Head

boys and, as with most friends you meet and make whilst camping and travelling, this was the last time we saw them. The boys added, however, that it was weird that they may one day meet these boys again and not know that they had met them before, or maybe even recognise them! But I reminded them, as they knew and had said themselves anyway, that that would literally be a chance of two in seven billion, so it was very, very, very unlikely.

MOVING ON – *Dad*

It was hard to move on from this tranquillity; it brought a little bit of faith in humanity back to me. Many people had been kind and helpful. Everyone had time to talk to other campers – it was almost as if everyone just wanted to stay at the campsite looking at the view, then talking and looking back at the view forever. This was a really unique place.

We did, however, have to continue on with the rest of our journey back down the western side of the country.

DAY 7 – *Adam*

On our first journey heading south, we drove alongside *Loch Lomond, which is famous for being the largest lake by surface area in Great Britain, with a length of 35 miles!* Whilst looking at this wonderful loch we saw many boats racing up and down trying to set speed records which made me think of the many speed records that had been set there previously. Then, minutes later we saw a man walking on the road, completely out of breath. Slightly worried about him, we asked him if he was ok. Turns out he was another man on a mission – walking from Lands End to John o'Groats. Sadly, he was on too much of a mission to let us know why he was taking on the challenge and he just wanted to push on! We bid him farewell, and silently prayed that he'd achieve the challenge given his current state of breathlessness! Trying not to worry about the guy too much, we rushed off in the other direction towards our next stop, which was for lunch near Loch Ness. Dad says he saw Nessie, but I don't think he did, he was probably just messing around with us. When we started having lunch, a man started flying a drone right over the loch. We wondered what he would do if it began to run out of battery and dropped into the loch! Whilst this was happening, his wife was taking pictures of numerous teddy bears that she'd lined up sitting on a stone wall – we still don't know why?!

After seeing this odd scene, we left in a rush as we had lost time over lunch. Fortunately, however, when we got to the next campsite there was enough time for us to play tag at the park with a boy called Will, which was very fun, but it came to an end as Dad called us in to go for a shower. After we came back and got dressed, we realised that we'd forgotten to bring back our shower gel so we rushed back to the showers and recovered it.

Finally, we read and then fell asleep quickly.

DAY 8 – *Dad*

Next destination – Ben Nevis! On arriving, I already felt that perhaps I should have planned to spend more time here to allow us to walk **all** of the glorious mountain. Who wants to brag to their mates, 'I only walked part of Ben Nevis'? So, although I knew we wouldn't have time, I allowed the boys to believe they could take on the challenge of getting to the summit. The three amigos, dressed for the challenge, set off with a bag of snacks, water and a map. Onwards and upwards, chattering all the way. But as the rain began to fall, it was clear to me that it was also going to be too wet and the visibility too poor to achieve the summit. Trying to explain this to an invincible nine-year-old who thinks he can conquer everything and anything was awkward. This was a time I needed Abby – for negotiation purposes. But she wasn't here, so I had to persevere and managed to seek out a compromise with him and that would be that we would one day return with Mummy and we would conquer it all together. Was he satisfied with that answer? Yes, at

Time for a swing near Ben Nevis

the time. But he's still waiting to return with Mummy to conquer the mountain to this day. Was the twelve-year-old bothered about not reaching the summit? Nah, it was too far anyway! So, we walked only about one quarter of the way up the magnificent path. Fortunately, there were breaks in the cloud so we were able to stop and admire the view, which was indescribable – even at only one quarter of the way up!

Eventually, after turning around to return, we made it back through the bewildering forest (trying out the rope swings on the way) which homed our campsite and back into our snug campervan where we played 'Pass the Pigs' for yet another time! Whilst this was happening, I thought about what we would be doing now if we **had** scaled the mountain – marvelling at the view, starting the descent or still climbing – but we had to think positively about what we had achieved instead. Because of this trail of thought, I lost the game of 'Pass the Pigs' and was stitched up with buttering the bread for dinner. We felt it was a good place to stay up late and play games, with the backdrop of Ben Nevis, so we did just that.

BEN NEVIS: THE FACTS – *Adam*

Ben Nevis is the tallest mountain in the UK, being an immense 1,345m tall, the path to climb the mountain is 10.5 miles. The quickest time to ascend the mountain is by Kenny Stuart in a time of 1hr 25 mins and 34 seconds. There are 2 main routes to the top of Ben Nevis and both tracks are dangerous. Once you have got to the summit there will most likely be snow and a great view waiting for you...

DAY 9 – *Toby*

JOURNAL Day 9:

Today we woke up to the horrible sound of rain showering onto the roof of the campervan. Adam and I got soaked when we ran to the toilet. Packing up meant that we all had to get soaked again, but, very soon, we were on our way to a small campsite on the edge of Glasgow.

We got very confused ~~as~~ when we booked into Mountain View Caravan Park because the man at the till said that 'they never take payment before arrival', but Dad was pretty sure that we had already paid, then we found out that we definitely hadn't.

Mountain View Park had facilities at the centre, static caravans on the outside and pitches in the middle. A little stream ran at the very edge, perpendicular to a very noisy train track.

After setting up, we took a quick ~~stroll~~ stroll into the village of Ambleside and had a lovely dinner of new potatoes, grilled spam and peas,

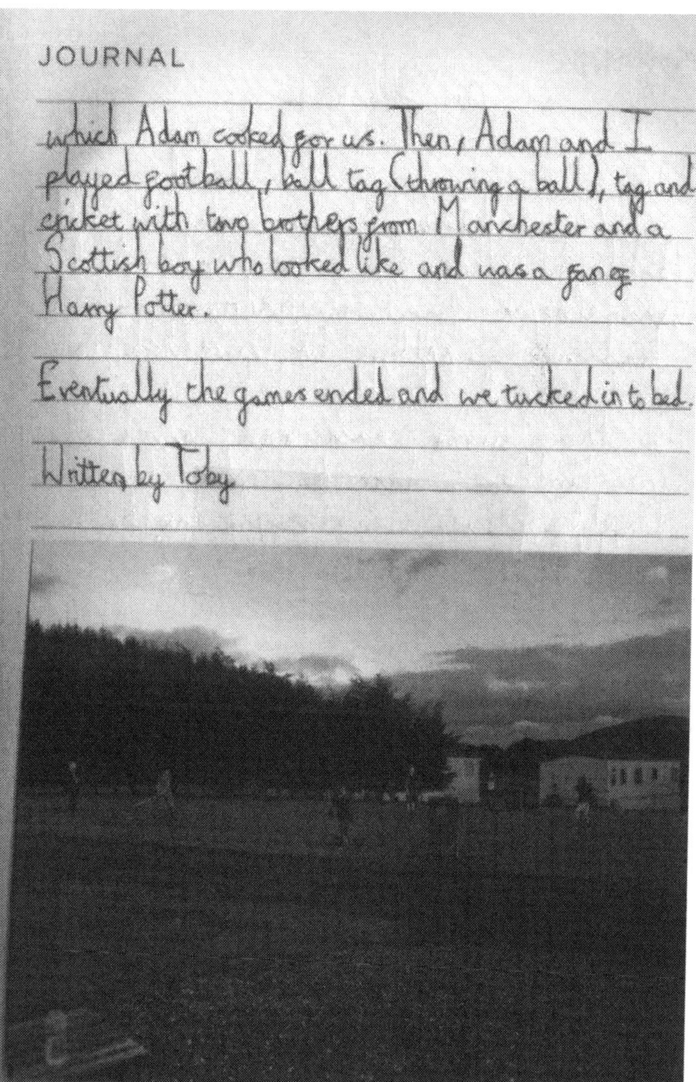
JOURNAL
which Adam cooked for us. Then, Adam and I played football, ball tag (throwing a ball), tag and cricket with two brothers from Manchester and a Scottish boy who looked like and was a fan of Harry Potter.
Eventually the games ended and we tucked in to bed.
Written by Toby

DAY 10 – *Toby*

We awoke early and got going straight away: we were excited to be heading to the Lake District. We were going to be returning to England once more, and that meant crossing the renowned Hadrian's Wall, which lay on the old border between Roman Britain and the Scots.

We stopped to visit the remains of a Roman stronghold along the wall. Although crumbling in places and with little of it actually remaining, the wall still seemed to stand impressively. From where we had parked to walk to a small history centre, it looked as if it continued on for miles!

The wall had been a political statement at the time, so it had been built with great effort and determination, whilst seemingly no fear about the cost of the structure. It was something to truly admire – our own 'Great Wall'.

Hadrian's Wall Photo shoot

HADRIAN'S WALL: THE FACTS

The wall, named after an emperor, was a massive structure. It took 15,000 people 6 years to build! They started building it in AD122 and finished in AD128.

Emperor Hadrian had claimed that he wanted to "separate Romans from the barbarians" to the north, who had apparently stolen from Roman markets, causing havoc. Roman soldiers guarded the wall as it was the only thing stopping the Scottish from invading.

Dad bought tickets to wander around the maze-like remains of the stronghold in an area that was now known as the Birdoswald Estate. Not much was actually left of the wall in this section, but it was clear to see from old architectural drawings just how huge the wall and the stronghold had been. We learned that where we stood, the wall had reached four-and-a-half metres in height and that there had been two three-story towers that had flanked two impenetrable oak gates. This was the West Gateway (or, in its Latin Roman name, the 'Porta principalis sinistra'). Roman soldiers would have guarded the gate around the clock, ensuring that only legitimate businessmen and traders passed through.

By studying the excavated remains of the stronghold, architects and archaeologists together, had drawn up a floorplan of the ancient structure. There had been a small blacksmith's workshop, for repairing swords, shield and other weapons. More spectacularly, however, was the remains of the sixteen metre by forty-eight metre drill and exercise hall (the 'basilica excercitatoria'), in which the soldiers had exercised and practised combat techniques. According to the educational signs and boards around the

Birdoswald Fort, this was the only drill and exercise hall in any auxiliary fort in the whole of the Roman Empire! No wonder it seemed so stunning!

As well as learning all this, we also found out that centuries after the Roman Empire had fallen, a Victorian family had paid for the employment of excavators and archaeologists. The family also built a medieval-styled house that is still there today, and is where we enjoyed a delicious lunch. A warm soup was what I had been looking forward too after a day's learning!

We returned to the campervan and continued on another long drive, heading to the Lake District, to a campsite close to Lake Windermere. For the last part of this journey, we were accompanied by the magnificent views that the infamous Lake District was known for, so I spent a lot of time gazing and admiring. We past plenty of huge lakes and endless forests, but we weren't the only people admiring the scenery, so we did, at one point, spend the good part of an hour winding around lanes, following a coach that had, for some reason, thought it sensible to drive down what seemed to be the tightest lanes in the country!

When we finally arrived, we played 'Pass the Pigs' once more and after tea, went straight to bed for a good night's rest.

DAD

We eventually ended up at the Lake District, another one of my favourite places. Growing up, I had experienced many an air cadet adventure trip to Windermere, later undertaking the Duke of Edinburgh expeditions here. The vast area to get lost amongst the flora and fauna amazed me every time; the covered moors and dense forests, beautiful lakes where all sorts of water sports take place. The home of Wordsworth and Beatrix Potter!

Whilst we didn't have time to do some of the incredible hikes or trek up Scafell Pike (again – maybe we'd return to complete the Three Peaks Challenge next time), we were going to go orienteering the next day, in the 24.47km² area woodland of Grizedale Forest, perfect in the rain under the thick covering of the woodland, bringing out the competitive side of us all. It's sad to think it won't be long before I can't keep up with them, as they get fitter and fitter!

DAY 11 – *Adam*

Orienteering: Dad guided and demonstrated to us how to get to the first Orienteering post in the forest, so we could get the idea and guide him to the next one. We soon realised what we had to do, so Dad didn't get to see the Orienteering map again! I decided to take us through the dense forest, much more fun and more risk of getting lost! Toby used the faster but longer paths. Dad says we did well but I wish we could have had a race: me versus Toby. Either way, when we got to the caravan we had dinner and then fell straight to sleep, exhausted!

JOURNAL Day 11:

Today we woke up at nine o'clock and lied in reading for half-an-hour. As usual now, we had a quick breakfast of cereal and set off. Today, though, we weren't heading to a campsite, we were heading to the nearby 'Grizedale Forest' for orienteering. Mum and Dad had done the same thing seventeen years ago for their anniversary. Upon arrival, we payed for a map and examined it in the cafe whilst eating steaming pasties and gorgeous sausage rolls.

Then the orienteering began. After jogging along a zig-zagging path, we entered the vast forest. We all took inturns taking the lead and very soon it got easier for us. Once, Adam lead us through an area of marsh and I ended up standing knee-deep in bog! Dad took us to one of the hard posts, which was at the top of a steep hill, surrounded by boulders. On the way back, Dad attempted to scare us, but we didn't fall for it. Sadly though, it was all over too soon. After playing in the park, we headed back to the campsite.

JOURNAL

We had a scrumtious dinner of hot-dogs and baked beans and headed into our cosy bed.

Written by Toby

P.S. Dad lost 'pass the pigs' again!

DAY 12 – *Toby*

During our long drive to Liverpool ('Li-ver-poool') I was so hungry, I took off my seat belt to pick up the lunch bag from the cabinet in the 'kitchen' where we'd put it for safe-keeping. Adam made a fuss about this being illegal and he ensured that Dad told me off. I was hungry and I wasn't going to sit and wait until the end of the journey to eat, but Adam adamantly disagreed.

It took us a while to get to Chester Fairoaks Camping and Caravan Club, but upon arrival we did not stop to rest, other than to set up the campervan. We were on a run in no time, knowing that our legs needed exercise. After twenty minutes or so, we returned and I was exhausted. The trip had, so far, taught us a lot of things about the UK that we didn't know at all, and this was no exception. Whilst jogging through as much of the area surrounding Chester as two young boys could in a little over twenty minutes, which in case you hadn't guessed, isn't much at all, we passed some remarkable sights.

Chester is very close to Liverpool and the rest of the Merseyside area, which all played a significant part in the Industrial Revolution which began in the North West of England towards the end of the 18th century. Throughout the industrial revolution, Liverpool became the world's leading city for cotton production, as well as continuing to experience a boom in its other industries – this did unfortunately include slavery. Because of this, its population grew quite rapidly from 6,000 to over 80,000 during the revolutionary period. Liverpool was – and still is – one of the most successful, valuable and renowned ports in the UK. It had links to other international economies and was a centre of trade for the UK. To share the growing business and wealth of Merseyside with the other powerful ports and cities in the country, connection routes were rapidly formed. These consisted of canals and railways, both of which we saw on our run. The evidence of Liverpool's industrious past remains, but not all in shape. What we could see were derailed ex-railway lines, no longer needed in as great a quantity as two centuries ago. In a way, it was somewhat upsetting to see that the once great structures were now in ruins, but what could be done?

After showering, Adam and I went to play football at the campsite's park and we joined another young boy called Noah, who seemed to be an insane footy player for his age (he was only 6 years old and and managed to beat me and Adam easily).

We finished off the day with a meal we were getting used to: SPAM, Smash and beans.

JOURNAL

Day 12

We woke early for breakfast in a moments time we were on ~~the~~ the road ~~had~~ heading for liverpool ~~(li~~ (li-ver-pool). On this drive, toby was being ~~illegal~~ illegal by not having ~~his~~ his seatbelt undone up. He did this to get lunch. When we got there me and Toby were aloud to play in the park! We made friends with someone called noah who was So Good At Football and he was only 6! After we went for a little walk/run we had dinner and went to bed.

Written by Adam.

P.S we had spam for dinner and the campsite was called chester caming and caravan club.

JOURNAL

CAMPERVAN-KEEPING (a.k.a. Housekeeping)

FOOD – *Dad*

I should perhaps mention that my fears for the trip had been of being an adequate dad and perhaps more importantly my promise to Abby, to feed the boys with enough healthy food. These fears had now been well and truly quashed.

Toby and Adam knew exactly what to eat. Yes, there were treats but they were well aware of the need to balance it.

We cooked plenty of food on the hob and grill – from SPAM, burgers, sausages, mashed potatoes, pasta, stir fry – they enjoyed doing it themselves; there was also a balance of grabbing the fruit that they had chosen when we restocked – grapes, apples, dried fruit (if that counts?) but they had taken to grabbing and munching on raw carrots too.

This is obviously down to the upbringing that Abby had installed in them. I was impressed by their culinary skills. They trumped any 'mess kitchen' hands down!

WASHING – *Dad*

I should perhaps mention, for those wondering, that the boys had also now become well-rehearsed in the 'one on, one in the wash and one spare' method of clothing, maximising the usage of shorts and t-shirts and the odd jumper. Whilst we were staying in those more luxurious campsites, every few days the boys enjoyed the novelty of inserting a few coins into a washing machine and tumble drier, ensuring they were kept fresh enough for any mother to be happy! Not to mention showers at most campsites kept them hygienic enough.

JOURNAL Day 13:

Today, we woke up early as we had a long journey through Whales to the Brecons, to complete. After the usual process of breakfast, teeth, and packing up, we hit the road.

We had snacks on the go, but, surprisingly, we arrived at Aberbran Fawr Campsite for lunch. After setting up, Adam, Dad and I explored the two fields, river and play park that made up the campsite. For Dad's benefit (as he'd been driving all day), we went on a walk/run along a public path. On the way back, we realised that there was a posh campsite and caravan club rally on the other side of the river to our campsite.

Today's dinner was very fun to cook: boil in the bag food. Dad had a steaming sausage casserole (the sauce was boiling when he opened the bag!), Adam hat pasta and pork meatballs and I had a tikka masala, which was almost as good as it is in an Indian restaurant! We all loved our main meals, but the puddings were disgusting. Dad and

JOURNAL

I had chocolate pudding, which tasted like rubber. Adam had toffee pudding, which was so hard, he couldn't cut it!

After our meals, Adam and I saved a tree swing (it was tangled in a bush), played tag with children who have permanent caravans on the campsite and also got taught how to use a segway! Then, we tucked into bed.

Written by Toby

■ Day 13 diary extract

DAY 14 – *Mum*

CATCHING UP WITH THE ROAD TRIPPERS

So, I'd managed to get through two whole weeks of back-to-back twelve-hour shifts at work whilst in the forefront of my mind the constant niggling and worrying thoughts of what my family were up to. I was pretty exhausted due to the long hours, but knowing that I had worked many hours of overtime to help fund the trip was exactly what I had set out to achieve. I'd lived on what I think of as student food – super noodles, jacket potatoes, baked beans and toast, as well as some hospital canteen food. I hadn't exercised much, as I couldn't squeeze it into the day. So, overall, I was feeling pretty lethargic. However, that feeling was completely quashed by the anticipation of catching up with my road trippers. My bag was packed lightly as there wouldn't be much room left in the van for my little luxuries. I had been expecting a list of items from Steve of things they may have needed to replace or things they'd run out of, but, to my surprise, they had managed with what they'd taken. Good planning, I guess? I locked up the house and made sure it was safe to leave, *following* Steve's instructions as this job usually fell to him. I'd planned to catch the earliest scheduled train – that way I could meet them as early as possible and have the biggest cuddles I'd ever had from them. Remembering that I had been without them for only two weeks, compared to long months Steve had gone without seeing them. I felt a little compassion towards him, but selfishly felt that my two lonely weeks had been an achievement!

The train was on time (*thank goodness!*), I didn't want to be a single minute late, I boarded and located my reserved seat. Looking around at the other passengers, I wondered where they were all planning on going – were they off to work, going to meet friends, going on a shopping trip? All the time I was hoping with anticipation that one of my fellow passengers would ask me what I was planning on doing! Had they asked, I might have completely overloaded them with my plans and what we had achieved as a family. I might have told them the places my boys had visited, what they'd seen and done. Sadly, no-one ever asked me, so my thoughts were kept to myself and my excitement built up as we stopped at stations and travelled through the country. The journey was pretty endless, it got busy at Bristol and then quietened down. My final destination was Cardiff Central. And there waiting on the platform, with big smiles, were the boys and Steve. It was **sooo** good to see them. The long journey had been worth it for the buzzing excitement we were all feeling! Toby was holding a lovely, yellow pot plant which he gave to me as a welcoming present – recently purchased at a TESCO store, where they'd been, en-route to the station, to stock up on fresh food, and by all accounts had taken advantage of the free fresh fruit for children that TESCO provide. It felt like I hadn't seen them for ages. They seemed to have changed in some way, but I couldn't really figure out why. Maybe their experiences and being with Steve had matured them in some way.

Cardiff Central

They were bursting to tell stories but the station was fairly busy and buzzing with trains coming in and out so we made our way to the car park where the boys led me to the van. They'd obviously made some effort to tidy it up to avoid any nagging from me. We climbed in the back and found room for my bag and a home for the plant, whilst catching up with each other – I didn't know who to listen to first, there was so much to listen to. It was great to be back together and it was clear that the trip had strengthened their bond, bringing them all closer together.

Deciding we should head back to the campsite, we had to choose our van seats. I wanted to sit with them all, but sat up front with Steve so we could catch up whilst the boys gladly sat in the back playing a game. Clearly, they were now released of their navigating duties and could sit back. Steve, glad of adult company and the relief of shared parental responsibility, visibly relaxed along the way. Whilst navigating through Cardiff (I won't go into detail about the bus lane, monitored by CCTV, that Steve drove into by mistake resulting in a small fine), we were engrossed in much needed conversation, so it didn't seem long before we arrived at the campsite which was very rural and sited next to a beautiful river. Expertly 'pitching up' the three of them demonstrated how slick the routine had become. It was just a few minutes before Steve had put the kettle on for a cuppa whilst I was given a quick tour of the site. It was **sooo** good to be with them all again, I'd missed them so much.

There were other children playing in the river and Toby and Adam were keen to join them. I had thought that they wouldn't have wanted to leave my side for a few days! I mean, if you were nine or twelve years old would you rather sit down and chat with your mum who you hadn't seen for two weeks or go and jump in a river, on a sunny day with other children, with dinghies and inflatable donuts? Feeling a little bit snubbed, I also wanted to discuss a few family admin matters with Steve, so I was equally happy to help them get their swimming gear out (neatly packed in their personal boxes – how had they managed to stay so organised?) and walk with them over to the river. Having had recurring nightmares, ever since Adam was born, of one of the boys struggling to keep afloat in deep, dark and murky water, letting them free in the river was a big step for me and probably always will be. But having only just arrived to join them, I could hardly prevent them from joining the other children who were all clearly having so much freedom and fun. They'd have wished for me return home again if I stopped them! So, in they went and as children do at campsites, they made friends quickly and were playing on the rope swings and sharing inflatable donuts. It was good to hear the laughter and chatter coming from the shallow river banks and river, but I couldn't stand and watch. What I don't know won't hurt me, right? So I left them to it and joined Steve outside the van.

Steve and I had a good catch up over a cup of tea. I was desperate to learn if the trip had been successful and if he'd achieved what he'd set out to achieve. To follow is my opinion on the success of the trip, I think Steve will be keen to tell his opinion later...

It was clear to me, even by looking at him, that he felt more relaxed than he had for a while. He told me that he had really enjoyed the whole experience with them and that they had all grown to rely on each other and had depended on one another for varying things. For most of their young lives, they'd mostly come to me when they'd needed laces tied up or help buttering bread for instance. He thought Toby and Adam had matured in independence as well, having had to deal with their own hygiene and care for their own belongings, while Steve had been sorting other things out such as final route planning, diesel checks etc. They'd had quality time together, not just doing fun things, but activities that just meant they were together ie. pitching up, planning walking routes, cooking meals. So, yes, on initial reflections, the trip had achieved what he'd aimed for. I was really, genuinely pleased (and relieved – imagine if the whole thing had been in vain!) for them all. Some might think, did I feel concerned that **I** may have lost some connection with them now? But I never once felt threatened by their now stronger bond and not once did I feel pushed out. After all, for the all the times Steve hadn't been around, I was their one constant. And that had been one point we'd always made when bringing up the children – that one of us would always be there. This was the main reason I had worked part-time whilst they were young; those hours had been as much school term time hours as I could make them (working in a 24/7 department, this wasn't always easy or welcomed and irritated some colleagues, but I did what I felt was right for my family). Yes, it put my career on hold for many years, but I was more focused on providing a stable home life for all of us, that's what made me happy. The career could come later, if I chose to pursue it at all.

Feeling reassured, I then felt it was time to bombard Steve with family admin/planning that had been ignored for the past couple of weeks. There were only a few minor issues, as I'd left the major issues at home! Things such as club membership renewals and beginning of school term time letters and future dates of weekend working to pop into the diary. All fairly boring and mundane stuff. However, going through all this with Steve, whilst sitting by the van, in an open and secluded campsite was relaxing and calm. The distant noise of the children in the background was in its own way relaxing, knowing they were having a fun time, feeling freedom from parental constraints. However, I wanted to see them again so it was time to retrieve from them from the river. Expecting the usual battle of not wanting to stop taking part in something fun, I was surprised when they gave in easily. Clearly, they were freezing, almost blue at the lips and uncontrollably shivering, so it was no wonder they were happy to come back to the campervan, grab their shower things and warm up in the onsite showers.

As this day was a special day, as we'd been reunited, we'd planned a barbecue on the site's firepit. The food, purchased earlier on their way to meet me, was prepared by all of us, working around each other in the van or outside near the firepit. It was simple food, but from what I could see, it was in large quantities. We spent a relaxed evening, barbecuing slowly, sitting around the fire as it grew colder. Steve and I enjoyed a nice bottle of red wine – Steve hadn't had a drop of wine for two weeks, so wasn't shy when pouring his glass. Clearly, he was in the mood to let go and relax! The boys chit-chatted all evening, and it felt so good to be together. Again, all good things come to an end, so I joined in their bedtime routine and we were all soon in bed and reading our books. When it came to lights off, I don't think it went as smoothly as it had been going throughout the trip, they just wanted to keep chatting and giggling! Plus, they were trying to terrify me with wild animal noises coming from the woods near the river, and stories of spiders crawling through the windows into the van. . .not the making for the best night's sleep!

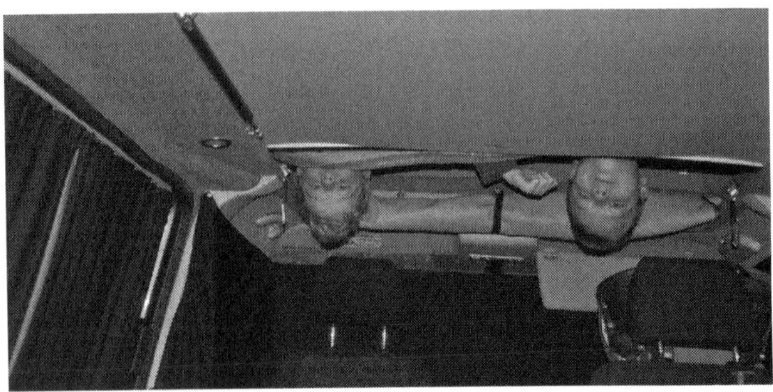

DAY 15–18

FINAL DESTINATION:

DEVON – *Toby*

So, with Mum now reunited with us, our final destination was Devon. We had a long, but fun, drive down south, playing the traditional long journey games i.e. I spy and teaching Mum the trip song: 'Despacito' – a song that was new at the time, but is now extensively well-known and enjoyed by many. Dad was more relaxed and had a continuous goofy smile on him, I guess that's because he now had Mum's help to look after Adam and me!

During these few days of Devonshire sun and sea, we were going to do so many exciting things! However, our stay was compromised when we got off to a bad start upon arrival at the campsite which was hugely disappointing as we had been so lucky with the condition of all the other sites we'd stayed at. Bearing in mind we were going to be here for a week, we were after a top-notch pitch! Top notch – it certainly was not! It was literally a mud bath due to the consistent rainfall they had been having over the past few days (which is weird because whilst we'd been in Wales, we'd not had rain at all, yet Mum and Dad have always said that it continuously rains in Wales. The two years they spent in St Athan, South Glamorgan, when Dad was posted there, qualifies them to say this apparently). Anyway, Dad couldn't park the van because it kept wheel-spinning in the mud! Brown sludge splattered up the sides of the van. We could all feel the tension rising in the van, like heat in an oven. Mum was trying to keep calm but with other campers watching, it was getting embarrassing. After numerous attempts of manoeuvring backwards and forwards and even sideways into the pitch, with Dad sweating buckets, the tension was about to burst, we gave up! Defeated, we drove to the reception. Dad politely informed the receptionist* that we had been given possibly the worst pitch on the campsite. Thankfully, I think she felt the vibes and without hesitation she kindly allocated us another pitch in the campervanning and caravanning section of the park, which turned out to be a much better standard of pitch (I think the receptionist secretly knew how terrible the first pitch was but had allocated it to us thinking we'd tolerate it. Little did she know we were experienced travellers now – so experienced and yet Dad couldn't park the van).

**Dad was actually really angry and I had been so worried that he was going to get snappy as I had seen him do before: when we first moved to Wiltshire, after Dad had been posted to a camp there, I remember having a Domino's and specifically, although I must have been only seven years old, I remember going with him to collect the pizzas. Whilst waiting in the takeaway's foyer, I heard one of the chef's swear and I then asked Dad if it was a rude word that I had heard. I now regret ever asking him this, because he suddenly steamed and flushed red and began slamming on the counter and demanding to speak to the manager, before shouting some more. The poor girl at the counter, who seemed very young, was taken aback (and Dad later found out that this girl was the older sister of one of my brother's best friends, which proved to be very embarrassing too!). The outcome was that we got our pizzas. The next day, Dad spoke to the manager on the phone, explaining the situation, and he agreed to send us discounts and vouchers as an apology. I don't know what happened to the chef, but I hope that he wasn't fired because of Dad's anger and I came away eternally embarrassed.*

The event at the campsite centre was almost very similar, but now I recognised the second coming of an angry Dad that I have only seen twice (thankfully!), so I urged Mum to tell him not to get annoyed at the lady at the counter, as it wasn't her fault that the pitch was unusable. I was even more worried when Dad said, 'We'll be leaving if they think that we can deal with this!' – I didn't want our stay here to be over straight away!

Although this had not been our finest hour, it turns out that all things have a silver lining. Dad calmed down as soon as the receptionist suggested the availability of another pitch and I breathed a sigh of relief – we would be staying here after all! Our new gravel pitch was spaced out and seeing as Mum doesn't really like sites where you are within ear shot of everyone around you, she was happy and therefore Dad was happy now too. We also had an electric supply and a water supply, but more importantly, the best advantage was that we were now closer to the beach!...

ADAM'S DESCRIPTION OF THE MUD BATH EXPERIENCE

Now, as the wheels were spinning, the tension rose – yes, everybody was getting grumpy and Dad was beginning to shout! I sat there listening to splodges of mud that were hitting the van from the wheels. I'd always wanted to do some form of fun activity in a car like drifting or a hand brake turn, but wheel spinning is not that high up my list. Either way it was good enough for me (now this was like what I'd seen done on Top Gear, one of my favourite TV shows). I sat there having fun: it was like sitting in a plane that is in the air but not moving backwards, forwards, or even down and up. Eventually Dad stopped taking his anger out on the accelerator and made off to take it out on the receptionist (sorry to her) except he held it back in the end...

BACK TO TOBY IN DEVON...

So Devon was the finale to the trip. We spent most of the week on the beach, sea swimming and surfing. We barbecued, picnicked and took some long walks along the beautiful cliff tops, absorbing the fresh air and views. Basically, we had been reunited with Mum and we felt whole again. To top this off, we were lucky enough to have our Granny visit us on Mum's birthday. She'd driven down from Somerset, with one of her infamous homemade Victoria sponges, disguised as a butterfly.

AN ICKY EVENING – *Toby*

(Please don't read this next section if you get queasy!)

Mum's birthday in Croyde involved not only Granny's delicious cake, but also fish-and-chips from the campsite's takeaway. It tasted good, of course, so all was well until Adam began to feel a bit ill. By this point, Granny had left to go home after spending the day with us, and Adam and I were preparing to go to bed. We had actually packed a two-man tent to take with us on the trip, in case, like on this night, we wanted to sleep outside. We had our walkie-talkie (to talk to Mum and Dad) and we had taken a bucket into the tent with us, because historically, when Adam says he feels ill, he usually is. We were both playing Top Trumps,

when Adam announced that he wanted to just lie down. He did so, but only minutes later, he said to me that he felt sick and it was then only seconds later that he literally grabbed and filled the bucket to about two-thirds of the way up with regurgitated fish and chips (which had clearly had something wrong with it). I haven't been sick in a very long time, so not only was I shocked by the stench to the point where I evacuated the tent, but I was also immensely impressed by the way that Adam had dealt with it. He had managed to get everything in the bucket, not a drop outside! He had also, immediately after finishing being sick, asked me in a matter of fact way to "ask Mum for some wipes", in the calmest voice possible. If it had been me, I would probably have been shouting for help! Adam had always been a sicky boy – Mum and

Dad always put it down to him being a 'Pye Baby' – he'd suffered from a pyloric stenosis when he was four weeks old and he had needed an operation to cure it.

JOURNAL Days 15-18 (Croyde):

On these few days of sun and sea, we did so many exciting things! However, we were badly shocked when we arrived, as our allocated pitch was a mudbath and the van couldn't park because it kept wheel-spinning! After Dad had politely informed the receptionist that we had been given a terrible pitch, we were moved to the caravan and campervan section of the park (we were first in the camping section). Adam and I put up a pup-tent and eventually we had set up camp at our final site: Ruda, which is in the surfing town of Croyde, in Devon. The site was jam-packed and the facilities were like public toilets, but it was in a great location. Our dinner was tomato pasta on the first day.

We got up at 08:45 on the second day because Adam and I were booked onto a surfing lesson at 09:30 until 11:30! Our teacher was an old, Australian man called Jag, who was bald and had a grey beard. He was hilarious and extremely encouraging. There were six others in our lesson - five were adults. Before entering the sea (which is actually

■ Day 15–18 diary extract

JOURNAL

the Atlantic Ocean!), we practised the technique, which Jae made easy to remember. Adam made it look easy by standing up on his first go, but I fell off the board and Jae told me that I had competition. Eventually, I managed to stand up! There were only two problems with surfing (both results of the beach being a surf beach): it was a tiring walk from the beach to the sea and the waves were battering me one-after-the-other. However, surfing itself is great fun! After bro-fisting and thanking Jae, it was sadly all over and we made our way back to the campervan for lunch. Mum and Dad said that they wanted a go at surfing, so later in the afternoon we hired surfboards and wetsuits for 24 hours. Annoyingly, we had to walk a long way down the beach again, but it was worth it. None of us managed to stand up, but we got close! We had spam, carrots and boiled new potatoes for dinner.

We got up late again on the ~~second~~ third day, had cereal for breakfast and then squeezed into our

PTO

THE BOYS' CONCLUSION

– *Toby and Adam*

The trip had fulfilled its aim. After growing up with a sometimes-absent dad, we had aimed to make up for the father-son bonds that now makes us stronger as a family. It does seem cringey for us to be writing this down, but it is true, we are closer to our awesome dad than we were before.

To repair the wounds of lost time, it doesn't require great wealth, or travelling abroad for weeks, or even to spend time over multiple years with the once absent family member. All it takes is three weeks, a good number of intense planning sessions, a beautiful country (your own country is always waiting to be properly explored) and true grit and determination.

DAD'S CONCLUSION

Our camping trip had taken months of planning and, as with most holidays, the build-up is equally, if not more important, than the holiday itself. Don't get me wrong, a last-minute weekend break can hold memories, but it is all over in a flash. The build up to family holidays can create discussion and bonds and can have a huge lasting impact. That is exactly what has happened here: the freedom to express and plan had allowed the boys to take ownership of the holiday. From this, they have developed and grown in themselves. Within the planning stage myself, Adam and Toby had a goal together and this itself was a great focus: bringing us together, and unconsciously learning about each other's needs – i.e. one of us would want facilities, one of us would not.

The mere execution of months of planning brings it all together and, in this case, shows what can be achieved when we all come together. Of course, memories were created and I felt closer to Adam and Toby after the trip. I realised how capable they had become and now appreciated them more for their personal characters and personality traits which, perhaps during our busy lives, I had maybe not fully cherished.

The trip was not lavish or expensive comparatively. We were fortunate that I had had a career and had completed enough time to leave the Forces with a pension. However, the same aim could be achieved with a lesser budget and we had indeed considered trains and camping in the planning. Contrary to this, a more extravagant option of hotels or going further into Europe could be considered. There are no limits to any budget, however, large or small it is.

In reflection this is something that will last for ever, maybe something to pass on or do with grandchildren, who knows? One thing is for certain, time does not stand still and our opportunities are limited with working lives, therefore the need to grab every possibility with the little people you have brought into this world is not timeless.

I would also like to thank Abby for her advice and support, in particular with parenting help. It was hard for Abby to be without the boys for two weeks and she threw herself into working extra hours for this time – which not only helped with money – but kept her mind busy. I think the build up to meeting Mum at the end was a great finale, allowing Toby and Adam to show their camping and cooking skills and share their experiences and not forgetting: we are one family unit.

EPILOGUE

We got through this immense trip successfully, however we did miss one target: we failed to reach the summit of Britain's tallest and most iconic mountain, Ben Nevis. As promised by Dad (on Day 8), we aim to return to the towering face with Mum (who we are *sure* would love to walk it with us); Date TBC!

ACKNOWLEDGEMENTS

The idea of writing this book was first thrashed around soon after returning from the trip. We all wanted to reflect on the whole journey and let families like ours know that there are ways of making up for lost time and opportunities for making memories. However, life got in the way and we didn't really attempt to write the book until last year (two years after the trip!). The drive for the book came mostly from Toby, who persevered and kept pushing us and pushing us to finish the story. The rest of us would sit and write the book when we couldn't think of anything else to do (not all being particularly fluid with our writing skills). Adam kept his contributions quick and to the point, a true reflection on his character. He was extremely keen to meet the publisher and discuss how much money could be made from the book!

Thanks Toby, for your determination. xxx

We'd also like to thank our family for all their help and encouragement.

Finally, we owe a massive thanks to Toby's school friend, Joe French, who designed and produced the front cover to our book.

Printed in Great Britain
by Amazon